LIFE & OMENS

Amtul Hajra

QUICK READS

by Writersgram Publications

LIFE & OMENS

Poetry by Amtul Hajra

First Impression: February 2020

© Amtul Hajra

ISBN: 978-9389244465

Published by: Writersgram Publications, New Delhi
Imprint: Quick Reads

www.writersgram.com
publications@writersgram.com

Amtul Hajra asserts the moral right to be identified as the author of this book.

*To the people who love me and embrace me.
To you and to me, with hopes we will reach
further one day.*

I'll leave the door open
and the lights on
In case you think
you got lost.

If things went her way, it could tear everything apart.
So she listens to you not to ruin things about.
Nothing ever goes the right way;
Even if she wants it to be.
May it be love, or the treaty of peace.

You as you; is all she wants.
She'll be her,
When you forget your frown.

Happy, she wants you.
"Please be" she pleads.

Time and again;
A spark is sure to be seen,

She's afraid for any fire to appea
If it does,
"It'll be the last of us you know."

The aftermath,
No you. No me.

Hate entangled; what love tangled,
Our souls are finally free.

All the time we acted like wannabe's,
And I was the only one that couldn't see.
Was 'fame' all you wanted in return of me?

They used to call us "perfectly paired",
Isn't it funny? But,
How are you going to pretend that you never knew me?"

❖❖❖

There's ice in my veins,
There's blood in my eyes;
When I cry, one of you is sure to die.

There's guilt everywhere,
But I'm too innocent for everyone to say.

I play with myself,
Learning everyday how to dive, and survive just fine.

There's hate in my heart; and love in my mind,
I'd blissfully give you all my heart,
Because all you'd get is hate.

My mind plays violins; the tune of sweet revenge.
The time when it was your knife, on my back.
Were pretty pitiful days.
Now it's my gun, and with your heart:
Is what I prefer to play?

Advising you to turn away wouldn't be of any better,
You've awakened inside of me: A deep violent hater.

Indeed, this isn't just my poetry;
This is my revenge.

"I'm happy, I'm happy, I'm happy."

Her heart, her mind
They play a game.

Is she really happy? Or is it just fake?

The mind makes getting to happiness amaze
The heart Keeps happiness Sound and safe.

The heart feels happy, seeing the beauty in the stars.
The mind debates,
'If he were here, he would call the galaxies ours'

(Heart): From black to white, giving me sight.
To see the beauty in you, in myself and others.

(Mind): Living on a greyscale, appearing so pale.
Crying out loud about things; doesn't matter even if they aren't true.

The choice is yours they say,
What's with choice?
If both of them are yours to say?

Staying; Seeking
Playing; Gaining
And giving what they've got.

Until The last inch of your Breath.

Sinking; Pleading
Bleeding; Drowning

Asking for help.

But none comes from the other side.
And your heart aches till its endmost breath.

You're Left with Everything.

And Yet Gaining Nothing.

Baby stay,
Tell me what you need.
It worked with you
Why didn't you pay heed?

To us, to love,
To silence and screams.

To madness, to sadness,
Where is the peace?

My peace lies with you
Yours?
I don't have a clue.

I've been yours;
You mightn't be mine.
Do you cherish the moments?
Of how often we dined?
Your place or mine
Everything so fine.

Our eyes that met,
My heart that fell
In love, for you.
Your character that fell,
In lust, for me.

Let me be convinced by,
Is this really true?

And here

My heart still asks you to,
Take me back to
From where we began

Let me kiss you

One last time

My pillow,
Is as light as a feather now.
My head is sinking,
And so my heart is.

My forehead is cold,
Enfolding the chilly
Thoughts;
UN controlled.

My vision is unclear,
My voice is unduly hazy.
My body is too craven,
No it's not easy.

The lights
Appear extremely abstracted,

A (my) soul
It's uncaging from the terrors of desolation.

Here I am,
Drowsing down;
Craving for a Felicity
Once more

Nevertheless,

Causing (all) this pain

Timid
And scared.
There I lie.

I can't breathe,
Nor can I tell you why.

I'm gasping for oxygen,
Like there's nothing more
I could lose.

I'm feeling numb again;
Possibly for the 100th time.

I endure a rush
In my veins,
The poison
Of anxiety running through.

I lay right there,
Till I pass out;
With the help of this
Only theory:

That "It was just a dream."

A Bad Dream.

❖ ❖ ❖

17:35

I have been cruel to myself,
Chasing thoughts in and out of bed.

There's light onto the floor;
It's the street light
A little far from my window.

I'm looking for you
But I see someone new.

I walk on my knees,
Sliding open the windows;
I scream and yell your name
I can't see anything
The tears filling my eyes are translucent too.

You are here, I can feel you.
You voice your heartbeat
Queer as it may sound,
I'm listening to it as you do.

I sit on the ground
Facing my window

let the moonlight breathe you to death, I'm falling I know. Only back into place.
Let the stars wave you goodbye. Hold me close before 18:00

A mouthful of sentiments
A mouth, Full of regrets.
A, mouth full of insolence.

My love: Mistaken
My words: forsaken
My cries are deepened.
My blood, is speaking.
For I am now Breaking.

Amidst,
This hollow of a world that cannot hold.

The burden of a soul
That pretends to its core.

The lava has been cooled down
With tears of my composure.

A mouthful of blood,
A handful of distress.
I'm mindful about the flood;
That's culminating my death.

I'm feeling highly human less.

❖ ❖ ❖

Stare into the void.
They call me paranoid.

Weeping Behind the curtains,
As soon as they fall.

Can't rest My palms
On the ground,
The shattered glass
Will pierce into my wounds.

Engraving the grief
Into the cracks of my skin.
Screams Overcrowd
The chambers of my Dark misery.

Dripping
Down my Anatomy,
The wine red Fluid;
Which defines my origin.

Writing;
With my own hands.

The story

Of how

I'll give up

On life.

❖ ❖ ❖

Murders, I caused?

I look into the mirror
I see a thousand ME's.

The knife I'm holding onto,
I rewind what happened in between;
Dragging along Trails of blood

It's not me, I know

Why am I holding on?
I hear screams and whispers.
Humming of the trees
The birds are out here

But why can't I see?

I can't help you, I'm sorry
I'm tired, maybe?

But I'm running behind
The horrors it's causing
Killing each one
With honour and applause.

The dungeons, The hollows
A place unknown.
It's dark, I'll follow
But where does it go?

I'm still, I'm quiet
Drifting to sleep.

Waiting
On another felony
It'll create.

En (chant) ed

Stating all the facts,
We both know to be true.

Nothing boring, nothing new.

Far away from the edge,
Close to the troubles I own.

Nothing boring, nothing new.

I crave to be the best,
I silence my inner self;
Drowsing into eternity of blues.

Nothing boring, nothing new.

Maybe champagne or some wine,
I think I'm allowed a few.
The daisies that fall;
From your fingers at 12
When I glance at your eyes
And yell.

You're broken, I know.

Are you the only one though?

Another phase, another decade.
Smoking a cigarette
In the middle of a maze.

Breathe in, breathe out:

Nothing boring, nothing new.

Dunking my head into the sink
I'll drown I thought
It's the end of me

Stars and sparks
What is this place?
I'm blowing away the darkest days.
I think I'm falling for you.

I pull the sheets over my head, there's darkness around. And suddenly it feels home
Darkness perceives of what I've been longing for, It's where I belong. Where I'm not
fearful. Where nothing can harm me. Solely, because I'm the only harm here.
Harm so murk, that grasps everybody it gets close to, and persecutes it to demise.

There's no getting back,
There's no forgetting.
It keeps me awake,
The iniquity.

It sweetly toxins me, And I'm off to a deep sleep.

At whatever time,
I get pulled back;
I'm prompted,

Prompted of the entire gloaming mystic.
And I'm inescapable,
Of all the despair.

I'm excessively unaware
Of all the agony it beholds.
That being, a reckless pair.

Disheartened, But faithful.
Accurate, But flawed.
Hostile But shambled.

Too much to complicate the shade,
And Too little to interpret hell.

Yet, Why?

Does this bring me tranquillity?
Why does this bring me back home?

Heavy rain and thunder on a dark night.

I have issues.
I loved heavy rain, I loved the thunder.
I loved a dark peaceful night.

But not anymore.

You ask me why,

Do I not prefer the black sky?
Or am I scared of the clamours the thunders make?

I give no reply.

But a thousand of them
Are floating around my head this time.
I was never afraid
Nor petrified

I am only reluctant, To the aftermath.

The aftermath:
The only thing that terrifies me.
Cause the demons Catch hold of me,
And here I am;

Letting my words flee.

They devour; my cast off Pieces.
Every inch of me, is still breathing.
Every promise I made,
Every chance I take.

Gasping for air, in awe;
At every warfare.

I'm not afraid, I never was
I'm the Delicate Virago.
Well built enough, But partial.

Anti-thesis

My heart eats up
Your sorrows.

I'm feeding on
Another one of your nightmares
That's causing you pain.

I lift you up
Like the lightest
Most definite form of love.

You're curling up under my hood
Softly.
You smell of grief tonight, my love.
Is this a warning?

You cry, and sleep. I weep and dream. You're glowing when the sun rises, yet my body is wrying.

Connecting myself
To the core of delight,
It just
Always
Refuses
To
Grant me
Purity.

Death of love

It must hurt
To finally know, what I contained.

All the time that I thought you'll comprehend.

You ask for forgiveness
From the paleness that you've caused
and of course you wouldn't know as we were paused.

We're in flames of carmine,
Watching our souls untwine.
And a woeful combat
Between both
Of our demons, Detached.

It must surely trigger,
Realising: the damages get bigger.
And I was a beautiful cave
For which you were allowed to pave in, your own path.

You dab, an amount of prestige
Onto your personality.
Splashing all the,
Insignificance over my
Unattended morality.

I've taken too,
Too much of heart;
Too much of soul.

As I give up blood,

I'm musing over you (Maybe) a last time.

I must alter my actions,
And turn them to you.
Now that we're done
I let you live as a slave
Cause the ashes that are deep buried,
The flames that burn with screams
Often unheard
May seem to be easily blown off
But it won't
It's wrath.

Lastly here I am,
Reconciling my words to you;
Putting them together
In and out of place.
The last breath I take (in your name):
Your honour, I rest my case.

(A beautiful poem penned down with Naba Naqvi, A friend.)

Tonight,
I need your help.
To remember who I am
There's nothing now that I've kept.

Weak and subtle,
Precious and dangling.
Far away from troubles;
You certainly look fancy.

The colour of my skin is melting now,
My bones are being moulded into something new.
My hand slips right through you,
And I cry "oh no, not again. This too?"

The windows of your eyes
Have been open for too long sweetheart.

Hum a tune
Go to sleep;
I promise you,
Believe me;
You aren't in too deep.

There's still time for you to breathe.

Di(men)sions

Sweet sins,
Of men i hear
Cruelly deceased.
To heart it's near.

My heart is diminished
Of earth that lie awake
At the hour of the dead.
Enclosed in a closet;

Warm but cool
Look at me, I'm the fool.

Step up, step down
Stir away the crown.
Of jewels and gems
Of gold and sins

Those you have committed
Abide them within.

Flowing over your empathy. Soft falling sympathy. Velvet-y touch of love, I'm longing for such a curb

vvv

Been long since that paled sunny sky,
Autumn winds are drifting by;
Magic moving under skies,
Never seen by waking eyes.
Except for them,
To those who believe,
Blissfully, beaming autumn vibes.
Dreaming as the days go by,
Dreamingly the summers die;
Eager eye and willing ear
A pleasing, wonderful tale to hear,
In autumn when the leaves are brown,
Reincarnating, a better one.
Take pen and ink and write it down;
Till the tale is rightly done

vvv

She looks around,
She feels the atmosphere;
The vibes
And the sounds.
Her Heart calls out the name
Her mind calculates about,
What is it?
Just a normal sunrise
Or a sun dawn.
The colours;
Bloom brightly
Confidently
And beautifully
When they hit her eyes.
The orange, the purple and the blue dyes.

The hues;
Of yellow of pink
Of grey.
The rays That Pierce past
The unwanted grim
Of every day.

the grey clouds of sorrow and despair,
The rays, constituting the inviolable you;
That cut across the uninviting torment.
And we still wonder where all the pain flew?

She picked up all the shades, she filled her heart
With genuine contentment: And not the one she always portrayed.

She,
Ultimately

Sleeps at night
Peacefully
Still
Untroubled and quiet.

There are people
Under the sea.
Solitary,
Miserable
And exquisite.
They keep concealed
The treasures
Beneath them.
The beauty
Of which
Is incomparable.
I've only caught
Quite glimpses of them
In dreams.
As you know now,
They like to be veiled
With the cloth of the sea.
Take me,
To the lighthouse
Which is built
In their heart,
And allow me
To Uncover
The pre-eminent
Pearls.

❖ ❖ ❖

Poetry was too good to be true,
Until
It was the only cease,
For the clashing of two;
Brutish souls
From the cluttering
Of ruptures,
Of my subtle existence.

I wonder,
I still ponder.
I wouldn't be here
If not for you.

Do I loathe you?
For giving me pain?

Or do I owe you?
For you taught me
How to form
Rhyming pairs
From my pain.

Once, what I used to
Believe it was you.
Now,
This is what makes me whole;
Poetry,
Is my home.

I write,
More than I speak.
I carry my words
In feathers.
They're silver lined
Like the moon.
I touch them with a
Light hand.
Fearing they might shatter too;
(My framework alike)
My idioms,
Are vague, unclear and appalling.
Sometimes,
Delicate and clumsy.
I sit retaining,
Each term of mine
Back to life.
It would be wrong of me,
To slaughter the one's
I'm hesitant of.
The courtesy,
And admiration (my) words deserve.
With all my heart and pain
I offer reverence,
To all (my) words;
Intense or plain.

I wish I could tell you,
Of all the pain and loss
I'm running through.
Keeps me from falling off;
I only float above the ground.

My pace is fast,
My heart doesn't follow.
It's eleven past,
Like wrecks between hollows.

Where am I to?
A map not known;
I'm willing to walk behind.
The ragged path forewarns me,
Tons of them are already entwined.
The shackles of sentiments engulf me;

Overdosing; recklessly.

And how are we told of?
An undying empathy.

Summariz(ed)

Holding up to another Sunday,
Relaxing in my armchair
With a book underneath my hands
And blankets wrapped around my feet.
The sun slipping through the mesh
And tapping onto my hazel hair.
The cold breeze dancing around me
I'm kissing the sorrows goodbye.
Daydream
About the fairies.
Almost hypnotic how I'm falling asleep.
An aura of hostility
Departing hastily
My body feels revolutionary;
Among sugar and honey
I'm unclear with what's more sweet.

Let's take a walk down the memory lane,
Isn't this our favourite place?

Houses lined up together,
In different colours
Being unique.
The tall and admirable
Properties,
Portraying architecture beautifully.

I wonder where Juliet
Must've been.
And Romeo calling out her name,
Among the whispers
Of the mankind.
Giving rise, to the eternity of amour

The lampposts,
You've always been amazed at them.
"The light is what you are"
You always say.

As we walk down the memory lane,
Sunsets happen each day.

Every colour of the sky
Reminds me of our goodbye.
There's a cafe,
At the end of the street;
The espresso,
Weaving our day complete.

High and proud,

As it stands,
Being the heart of the city,
The Eiffel tower is much
Ladylike.
The wind softly swifts,
Through the trees
And birds fly soaring into the sky.

The vile of love,
People, so kind and sweet.
There's poetry buried
Deep in these usual rose shaded streets.

What was her favourite colour?
Was it the brown in your eyes?
Or
Was it the pink in your smile?
Was it the black that you so often wore?
Or
The red that you adored?
Was it the blue that reflected through your eyes?
While watching the sky changing dyes?
Or
The Green that's twinkling,
While you're presenting me flowers tonight?
Was it the vibrant orange turning to violet?
When you come home to me, smiling; that makes my heart go silent.
Or
Yellow, the colour of butterflies that flutter when you make me smile.
Was it White that represents my peace within you?
Or
The gray, that showed me your timeless love none could undo?
Was it silver?
Or was it gold?
The colour of your Heart
And
The colour of your soul.
Was it-
Her favourite colour was you.

One year later, I'm still where you left me.
Tired, undone and unfinished.
Untangling the knots
Of disappointment.

Two years later, I'm halfway there,
Still holding on,
To the promises you made.
Nearly forgetting,
You were never there.

Three years gone,
There's love for me to feed on.
Roughly recollecting the sense
Of your touch.

Four years lost,
There's so much I've gained.
Strength and happiness,
Unduly maintained.

Five years remained,
I've lost count now.

Too busy enumerating,
Favours of people
Who've loved me?
Helped me,
And embraced me.

Tell me,
What won?
What gave in?

Amtul Hajra

Unkn(own)

I've been to far off places,
Not one of them were as queer as you.
You're like a strategy dug so deep,
I sense sadness when I hold you
Melancholy, at the brim of your throat;
Like a place I've not known.

The words pouring out of your mouth when you speak,
How you call my name,
As pleasant as a melody.

At 3 am.
The creeks of your body tell me stories,
Of war and ruins;
Of love and peace.

You taste,
Like Light and grief,
And dark happiness that's clinging onto your lips.
The madness that's growing on you;
When you watch sunsets each time,
With the sea rushing on your feet.
How you feel the wind crashing on your skin,
And I silently listen to your heart crack;
As you close your eyes,
And hold my hand

I enter into the world you own.

No (cry)ing in the club

I'm healing myself
Crying out loud.
Stitching up wounds
They have been open for too long.
 For days and hours,
Melancholy and solitude paves way:
"Stray" I say
"Go away"
Covering myself up
With hopes and desires,
New.
With diamonds and pearls,
Singing along to a different tune.
Smearing the wine red fluid onto my lips,
Putting on a new shade of soul:
Music as loud as the thunder
This time. I won't break down.
Whirling and swaying
As tears wash down my mascara,
I'm ending this woeful era.

The final call

Look up at it like it's the most beautiful thing,
And when it's not around…
The most dreadful thing ever.
Hold it down, show it off
Try to come up, let it down.
After all. It's all have had enough.
It'll come up,
It'll let you down.
You'll see when it happens about.
And there's nothing that could ever stop,
Because when it's started it can't be put to a stop
Let it get you, for a moment.
Let it poise at invisible.
Because none could ever see it,
Then why you?
Stay where you were,
Stay how you are.
Won't you be the one to end it all?

Relapsed Fears

They never ask you to play?
Are they inside you?
So silent and stay?
To be, there is.
To not; there isn't.
For you; there is.
For me; there isn't.
Deep down the light
Shallow above the dark.
Pleading for them to go away
Only' they don't prefer going off
For I
Love them too much
To shoo them away.

We sway, we swing
In our own axis.
Too wild to last
Too rare to break
Binding the blind imagination,
The only weapon against reality.
Wrapping our devils
Putting them to sleep.
They fly; they flee
Absurdity capture our dreams
For despatching our enemies.
Running through spirals
Fading through titles;
Reaching a land
Of faded happy vials.

A Painting

I dip my brush of Integrity
Into the faithful
Colour of merriment.

I wet the canvas of misery
With the water
Of despair.

Then I place
The colour of merriment,
On the canvas, pervasively.

Next comes
The silent colour
Of imagination.
With it,
I paint skies
Among Delight.

Then there's
My brush
Of cowardness,
Bit by bit
I dunk it
Into the wicked colour
Of adventures.

I paint with it
The houses and the trees.
The forests that lead
To journey's too deep.

Then there's my
Time-worn brush Of Love,
Every whirl of which
Is twisted and turned.
However,
It's the most Eminent
Of them all.

I coat my love,
With the colour
Of
Generosity,
And hope.

With
Infinite care,
I paint my base.
(The land beneath,
Which I stand upon)

The last brush of
Harmony and solitude,
Coated with
The melody of
Long-lasting hues.

I draw,
And fill.
Flowers of all kinds,
They deliver
Freshness
And an up vibe.

There's the art,
Now it's up to you.
To picture
What it conveys to you.

Every day is a painting

I'm the artist
Emotions are my colours,
Every minute is my canvas.

After every ruthless night in tears,
Everything is better in the morning I suppose.
To try and try till the lights go off;
Only to end up in the very first line.

We fight, we fail
We learn, we inhale
We climb to the top;
And shout out 'checkmate'
We don't stop
We aren't late
We're warriors till our last breath.

I fell through the cracks
Of my stories,
Only to reach the everlasting
Joy of poetry.

Tuck me under the waves,
Let the soft white sand be my pillow.
The creatures, my friends,
The reflection of the sun, my happiness
And the flora my dreams.
Leisurely,
I descend
Into a
Moist
Fresh
Chilly
And gloomy entity.

There's nothing more charming
Than the scent of the angel holding me
Securely; tenderly
And with all the love he owns.
Never letting go.
The thought of goodbye,
Reminds me
How deeply I fear
Separation.

My eyes drown,
In water then.
It's not the sea or the ocean.
The lies you gave,
The trust you broke,
You left me;
So that I could die in those.
And then you come;
Pleading again
Saying sorry for what you caused?
It's just all your facade.
A broken heart,
A million pieces,
All you did was put glue:
This washed away with no clue.
You gave me warmth,
Left me cold:
Like the dead without a soul.
Left me alone,
In the middle of the sea
With an anchor tied to my feet.
I see no hope of me,
Nor will you ever come and save me.
I went blind with rage;
Crying all my age.
You flew away,
With the happiness we shared
Leaving all the bitter memories there.
A smile on your face,
With no trace of remembrance;
You had no mercy,
You told me you had pity
On me, for choosing you

That I couldn't even foresee;
All the pain you could cause me.
You left scars,
Which wouldn't stop bleeding,
And took my heart,
Which never stopped pumping
You crushed my heart
With your bare hands,
Turning me into a demon
Of the seventh hell.
All of this?
Just over a night trust me!

(A profound poem, written along with SAK, a friend and companion.)

So, adore yourself
The heart that strives you the most
Is the heart that lives withiin you.

Carry it with tenderness
And treat it with all the sweetness
You own.

All the nectar
Of the flowers youve sown,
Will soak into your spine
And align your throne.

self-love